BILL OF RIGHTS

BILL OF RIGHTS

Fred D'Aguiar

Chatto & Windus
LONDON

Published by Chatto & Windus 1998

2 4 6 8 10 9 7 5 3 1

Copyright © Fred D'Aguiar 1998

Fred D'Aguiar has asserted his right under the Copyright, Designs
and Patents Act 1988 to be identified as the author of this work

First published in Great Britain in 1998 by
Chatto & Windus
Random House, 20 Vauxhall Bridge Road,
London SW1V 2SA

Random House Australia (Pty) Limited
20 Alfred Street, Milsons Point, Sydney,
New South Wales 2061, Australia

Random House New Zealand Limited
18 Poland Road, Glenfield,
Auckland 10, New Zealand

Random House South Africa (Pty) Limited
Endulini, 5A Jubilee Road, Parktown 2193, South Africa

Random House UK Limited Reg. No. 954009

A CIP catalogue record for this book
is available from the British Library

ISBN 0 7011 6525 1

Papers used by Random House UK Limited are natural,
recyclable products made from wood grown in sustainable forests.
The manufacturing processes conform to the environmental
regulations of the country of origin.

Typeset by Deltatype Limited, Birkenhead, Merseyside
Printed and bound in Great Britain by
Mackays of Chatham PLC

For Debbie

ACKNOWLEDGEMENTS

Parts of this poem have appeared in *Heat* (Australia), *Kyk Ova Al* (Guyana), *Poetry Ireland Review*, *Callaloo* (USA) and *Poetry Review*.

Thanks to Sony Music Publishing for permission to quote from 'Lay Lady Lay' and 'Señor Señor Can You Tell Me Where We're Heading' (words by Bob Dylan – Special Rider Music/Sony/ATV Music Publishing).

Thanks also to Benjamin Zephaniah for the use of lines from 'This policeman keeps kicking me to death'.

From Chattanooga, from Brixton (L—, write),
From hallowed be Thy name, Thy kingdom come,
To the Potaro, Essequibo, Demerara,

From 132 gradations – blue-black to chalk-white,
To watch-that-sun-and-overproof-rum,
The sweet potato, bow and arrow warrior,

The near one thousand came and stayed.
I am your saviour. Follow me. And we did.
And planted, did we plant, on a hill;

We sang, clapped hands and prayed
For rain, for our cutlass to miss us as we weeded
Before now tending a pot on a window sill;

And the rains came and washed the crops away.
And we planted them again, and they were
Washed away, again; and starved, we starved,

Calling God, Allah, Jah, and Yahweh
Ease this belt tightened to a notch where
None existed, one a hot knife tip carved;

Until the locals took pity on us.
There were, after all, pregnant women,
Children and the very old, in our midst.

They brought wood treated to take this sun,
Zinc as sound as that ship of Nemo's,
And a smile with the force of a blitz.

'Occupancy limited to 118 persons.'
We sat in the aisles, plunked children
One on top of another, into laps,

Volunteered for the cargo hold
And would have remained there
As directed by Father had the pilot

Not said we'd freeze or suffocate
At 33,000 feet, or both, I am among
The agile ones, curled in the overhead

Luggage compartment.
                                        A mercen-
-ary maybe, archvillain
Certainly not; whatever label you slap

On me sticks like Velcro sold
At Woolworths at sixpence per square.
A paper-round meant you could buy lots

And be popular in the playground at break,
No longer the butt of classroom jokes – a gnome
Whose head got rubbed, called dear, dear-e, dear-e-o.

Goodbye Chattanooga. Hello Potaro.
Later, L— and Brixton. Essequibo, here we go.

Someone they call a buck light-footed
It over to me. I jumped but his open palms,

A stupid smile and his near-naked frame
Put me at ease. He gave me corn

I bolted down. His head shake, finger wag
And suppressed chuckle told me I'd done wrong.

This is not a portion of potato
Chips wrapped in salt and vinegar – what a hog! –

Wrapped in turn in yesterday's news, that suited
Me fine for supper, that went down a charm

Chased with a can of shandy and a shame-
-less belch close to speech, full of scorn

For having to chew each mouthful sixteen gawd
Awful times, virtually digesting it on the tongue.

Dip the tip of an arrow in this plant sap,
Let it dry, untouched, in the sun,
Let it fly into that wild boar.

Roast the boar but offer some to the sun,
Carve buttons from the bone,
Dry the skin, tell the boar you are sorry

But you have a thousand mouths to feed
And it fits the bill exactamundo.

Add to these plant sap
Taste of a tangerine sun
Wild in the meat of that boar
Roast from that aluminium sun
Buttons in those bones
Eyes in those buttons you tell sorry
Thousand mouths you have to feed
A thousand grins feeding you
Bill that boar fits exactly

Bow tie, bodacious, Father. Model divine Daddy.
Friend of Lenin. Friend of Amin. Friend of Stalin.
Here the Trades rinse the air constantly.
Rain returns the verdant to grass, trees and paling.

'All the days of my life, ever since I been born
I never heard a man speak like this man before.'
1000 Tarzan yodels tear the night to ribbons.

Night flutters in the breeze in shreds
Cries strike the dark with the spark of fireflies
To wave a mosquito from the forehead
Takes more effort than to clear this forest
Clear this continent of all of its wood
Burn that wood into smoke into cloud
Spread that cloud over the entire planet
Sink our planet into a black hole
Send that hole spinning into unknown space

Holy is coconut with cream and water
Holy stinking-toe and sour-sap and eddoe
Holy this vision in Him that brought us here
Holy His name Jones and His every aspect

Holy am I for my proximity to Him
Holy this Uzi blessed in service to Him
Holy every drop that rains and rusts our joints
Holy the hard wood greenheart in these huts.

Holy Him holy me holy you
Holy this holy that holy de-tarat!
Holy the serpent of temptation
Holy Pontius Pilate holy Judas Iscariot

Holy this sun uncut through rain
Holy the Buckoo Jumby Ol' Higue
Holy that giant pearl elasticated on water
Holy water gyrating underneath that weightless jewel

Autochthonous wood.
Purpleheart and greenheart
Blunted or broke electric
Saw after electric saw

In half. Wood this tough
Cannot have known much love
And must have hardened itself
Against further loss of face.

Against further time loss
Against further body loss
Against further mind loss
Against further soul loss
Against further blood loss
Against further life loss
Against further loss

In Chattanooga as in Kalamazoo
We had three square meals, inside loos
And an inside to speak of.

Here in paradise, Essequibo, Potaro,
The branch's leak never switches off.
I have the runs and chigoe,

A fungus culture between my toes.
I patrol this new town's perimeter
With my finger on an Uzi's trigger.

Rain our metronome
Rain our gait
Rain our habits
Rain our wake-up call
Rain our lullaby
Rain our flotilla
Rain our love
Rain our life
Rain our whore
Rain heaven
Rain hell
Rain God
Rain Devil

Yoknapatawpha county,
This was not.

Rice for breakfast,
Rice water soup for lunch –
Yes there was time for lunch –
Rice and beans for dinner,

With the stubborn giant anteater,
The sloth and the caiman,
Too tough by far,
Even for our meagre pots.

In this dream
There's no word for rice
No picture for rice
No taste for rice
No smell for rice
No touch no sound
No imagining rice

Topsoil gone in the rain with our seedlings.
Spirit for fighting back this wilderness gone
Too; all that's left unencumbered is my love
For Father: my nerves are a Stradivarius

In the hands of a musical pygmy.
Inside I sound like cats in an alley
Mating or squabbling over a smell of fish.
My face is as expressionless as a satellite dish.

Fingertips gone
Thumbprint too
Heels bone sore
Toes stiff stumps
Palms raw
Instep raw
Knees can't bend
Not even for God
Nor land nor flag
Not even for Father

Flint flicked into flames.
Two sticks, greenheart or purpleheart,
Rubbed together until they catch.

Our matches are moist and useless.
Kerosene wicks drown in the mist.
The vines are flame-shaped,

Cold and green as moss. Leaves leap,
Curl, crawl as if out of control.
Their razored edges cut and burn.

Razor grass moon
Flint stick sun
Needling rain
Obeah moon
Witching sun
Stone rain
Laser sun

Brixton market was rough but this is rougher.
I could find saltfish and eddoes near the reggae
Shop that shook my fillings and made my ears ring.

A 37 bus always came eventually –
Often after a long wait – in twos and threes.
And at my council flat there was a hook

Behind the door and a jabbering set
That snowed, drizzled, then cleared after a thump.

Chump chump went the piranhas
On the children who jumped
Unthinkingly into the river
During a spell without supervision
Oh red river
Howls under water
Blood signalling miles downstream
For more, more piranhas to come feast

The Front Line can be scary
But the banks of the Potaro are scarier.

I used gum on a stick to capture a canary,
Locked it in a bamboo cage and waited for its aria.

But it stayed dumb and I grew hungrier
And hungrier, caring less for its song

And more for its meat, and succumbed
Losing most of the meagre roast to the griot.

A man pulled a knife on me for stepping on his alligator shoes
Another saw me ask for change on a street corner and thought
I was moving in on his turf to push weed of my own

The only weed I know pushes through concrete fourteen storeys
Up the sides of my council flat tower block
Come sun rain gale sleet or snow

What a feisty griot! He talked with his mouth
Full and told his story in instalments,
Silenced by morsels of that canary.

I went without for a story full of the warm South.
That griot didn't even leave me bones.
He chewed them to powder;

Except for one bone which he hollowed
Into a flute and played and lulled me to sleep.

What canary bone?
Human more like!
Weren't we fine young cannibals?
Seeing a canary as we munched
Instead of you or me
Made swallowing easier
Or else the jaws would have clamped
Down seized-up locked shop jammed shut

Not a dreamless sleep, one with nightmares.

Men, women and children queue before a pot
More like a vat and drink or else are shot,

Their cries that could raise the dead, raise hair
And a thousand flutes in a death air,

A thousand flutes piled on top
Each other, like so many grains of rice.

Trained on a meandering line of souls
From Brixton, Chattanooga and Kalamazoo,

Was an Uzi, I knew, held the way I do.

A thousand flutes for bullets
A thousand souls for flutes
A thousand bullets for souls

I woke with Cassandra Wilson's Tupelo
Honey on my mind and a snapshot –
Me guarding our reverend leader's pot
Of plenty with my finger on my trusted Uzi.

Drink, I was ordering them, Drink,
As I tapped out that tune on the trigger
When my head cleared it was the reverse –
One of those Kodak Instamatics and silence.

Silence except for the baying of the blood
Silence above the wind in the trees
Silence as the river breaches its banks
Silence of us like fish in a tank
Silence in the lengthening plait of vines
Silence so that Father can catch forty winks

Nails driven home with rubber hammers
Teeth flying from a bandaged fist
A headlock until somebody or other goes limp
Hands over the mouth and nose until some face blues
All ship-shape while Father gets his shut-eye

From planting on a hillside
Under an unsheltering sky
To banana leaves for a roof
To these shingled wood huts

Took time, but we had help
From a government, tribes,
And God like a man in our midst
Telling what came to pass.

What came to pass
Has come to pass
Has come and gone
Came and went

What came to pass
That has not always passed
Already came and passed
What comes must pass

What came to pass
Came and did not pass
Did come did pass
Had come had passed

What came to pass
Came to stay with us
Came in fact for us
Came and we passed

There is a relevant passage in the Good Book
For this season of pestilential rain
For our crops that refuse to grip hills

For the mosquito that sings as it sucks us dry
For watersnakes, manatees and marabuntas
For the hours when we huddle for warmth

For nothing no thing catches to make fire
For our God who preaches patience
Who by example starves and falls into a fit

That relevant passage slips my mind
Slips from the Good Book
From this rain forest
This wet world
From this moment referred to as
That slippery passage
That irrelevant passage
That not-so-good Book
That so-so Book
That kiss-me-arse Book
That rain rain that never fucks off
That world beyond this arse-hole forest

The Reverend has a propensity for virgins.
They're hard to come by in this wretched jungle.

After dey is pregnant for him we get them as wives
All our firstborn are the children of God.

If they get any younger it'll be pederasty.
Touch a girl before he does and you're dead.

So we give it to them up the arse,
Channel B we call it, Channel A is for the Super.

Boys are not spared
Wives are not spared
And if those goats stood still
For long they too would not be spared
Spare not the rod . . .

Bearded vines clutch at ankles,
Hands and heads. Streets here are wind-
Made or water-travelled; not for foot.

Our feet are winged by our faith.
We rip those vines from their roots
Even as they rip our flesh off our bones.

We feel our faith bolster with each test
So feel nothing: doubt are the worms
We pull for each other from our flesh.

Pull and eat
Pull and cry
Pull and lay down and die
Pull and multiply
Pull and try not to break
Pull and faint
Pull and pull
Till we can't pull anymore

I was there
When Jones cracked
His one and only joke

He called Guyana's
Bracken-tumbling
Savannahs

Blasted
Flat-arsed
Country

Such exaggerated
Ceaseless laughter
As there was

The likes of which
Had never been heard
Before or since

In those jungle
Confines curbed
Only when Jones

Failing
With his hand
Held high

And repeated
Dismissive waves
Suddenly

Lost his temper
Pulled off his belt
And beat everyone

Within reach
Ignoring his trousers
Around his feet

I can testify
The man never wore
Any skids

Or underpants
Swing low
Sweet chariot

Father, this well too deep.
This well too dark, Father.
Big hands and feet, push me
Under water, Father.

Give me your purpleheart
Or greenheart stave to this
Father; a stinging lash
That when it's over, it's

Over; but I carry
This water for days, Father,
After that night, that well
Never leaves me, Father.

Water in the well
Till the well run dry
Is not the truth I a-tell
Is pure lie
Lie pure like water
I a-tell

If the R's could see their daughter
Now. A lady in waiting. She hath drunk
Honeydew for too long and tasted . . . not!

Coffee's ghost lingers among the vines
And that snake doubling as a bird is Quetzal-
coatl, in those vines swinging from tree

To misted tree, vines my cutlass
Bounces off. Lay lady lay.

Daughter of the revolution
Daughter of the dust
Daughter of the water course
Daughter without a past
Daughter born big so
Daughter born voluptuous so
Daughter born wise so
Speak to us

I went on a recce,
Up the twisting Rupununi

All the way to Karaudanawa.
Mist stopped my Seiko.

Suddenly, I was hard for punani.
I unzipped and waved my banana

At the dense trees like a gekko
Whose nerves have been on a rack.

It takes a little and a lot
To turn a man into a mouse
Reduce him to a louse
Banish him under the house
Like a mangy dog
Shoot him for grouse

Savannah, raced by bundles of bracken,
Raced by the uninterrupted wind,
Raced, in turn, by someone, equal in stature
To the Reverend.

God is in His heaven.
The People's Temple know Him as a statue
That comes to life with the wave of a wand
In the form of our Jim, that can't be broken.

As the savannah races towards the forest
The forest retreats towards the river

As the river reaches for us
We plant with our backs to the trees

The savannah knows God watches
The forest knows it too

Yet the savannah advances
Still the forest beats its retreat

Someone's wife, she was Waiyaki or Makusi.
She said she washed her waist-length hair
On the stony banks of the Mazaruni.

I doubted her; not. She thought I resembled
One of C.L.R.'s Black Jacobins. I trembled
With unadulterated lust, not for her,

But for handfuls of her hair and the rest
Under us like an eiderdown in our love-nest.

Someone's wife is always sweeter
Makes you want to grab and eat her
Standing sitting lying down
Frontwards backwards round and round

Someone's wife is someone's traitor
Another's boss secretary neighbour
Standing sitting lying down
Frontwards backwards round and round

That long-winded start to Gershwin's
Rhapsody in Blue is how she sounded,
As we lay on her hair, in what was not jazz,
So much as our own private mashmarami.

Somehow her husband must have caught wind
That she was up to no good, with no-good
Boyo here, less Romeo, more Mack the Knife
Armed with an Uzi, I asked her to marry me.

With her husband in the picture
Things were bound to take a turn
From superb to let's say not so good

My heart was quick for her
But with him in the frame
I was close to a myocardial infarction

Not in a mood for any Bruce Lee antics
I pointed my trusty steed and pulled on the reins.

It reared and shot off. He fell among the ants
By the left bank of what could pass for the Rhine

A muddier version; a browning version.
She produced her Gershwin, but Handel

I could handle. I knelt and kissed her ankle,
Put my Uzi in her hand and bowed my head.

In suppliance to you
In solitary to you
In the dog pound to you
In slavery to you
In abdication to you
In death to you

I'm still here . . . but for a while
Doubt had me there, she seemed to consider,
At least for a moment, squeezing that trigger
But she lifted my chin and I saw her smile.

All I had to work out with her was that she
Was a virgin, and I was bringing her to him,
Like a kind of offering, then she could be mine
And stay with me, in our budding El Dorado.

Stay with me through thick and thin
Through worship and sin
Through birthing and killing
Stay with me and I'll stay with you
Through red white and blue
Through dreadlock gridlock matlock too
Stay with me don't bother with him
We're at the beginning so let's begin
If it helps pretend I'm his twin

Captain Steadman faced the same conundrum
Two centuries ago. Two centuries later
We could surely triumph. We had swapped the drum
For the telephone; the leech for the vaccine.

The Reverend was right, of course, adversity
Should make us stronger, but his proclivity
For virgins is aroused by my girl's obvious
Plural virginity, each of which he spends

Several days taking again and again.

There's a part to my darling
Even the Reverend with his probe
Can't reach however much he tries

I get no solace from this piece
Of knowledge no shut-eye
No dry-eye no dilated pupils

Beep-beep, sounds the empty jeep.
I feel like Coyote, always out of reach
Of Roadrunner as I watch it overshoot

This commune, this town surrounded by jungle,
And I let off a round from my gun
And a few colourful birds drop

Like manna. The truck carries on
Beep-beep. A coconut caught by my Uzi
Just misses my head with a loud plop.

Coconut why you miss?
Why you don't knock me dead?
Why not split my head
Scrunch my nut
Crush my egg?
Coconut you playing with me?
You take me for a fool?
Your tool?
Your plaything?
I am a man.

I took the safety catch off my Uzi
For a test fire and found the damp
Had got to it too. I threw it down
And it went off like a charm.

For each round that I spent wantonly
I was fined. I had to see Father,
Himself. He laid a hand on my shoulder
And delivered a sucker punch that floored me.

Either I have a glass jaw
Or Father is blessed as a boxer

Or maybe when a God hits a man
All a man can do is drop
To his knees and beg for mercy

Damp everywhere seizes my Uzi.
I am arthritic at thirty-three.

Come back Chattanooga
Heidi-ho Kalamazoo;

The Potaro, Demarara and Essequibo
I don't know, I can't know, not now.

There is river water in everything,
And what the river can't reach is left to rain.

Rain water collected in rain barrels
Rain water pumped with generators from huts
Into rain barrels into rain
We boil the rain and the river
Before we drink either
Both give us gripes
We hate both in equal measure
Both rise and fall on us
Without warning or consideration
Without so much as a say so

If I was in Greenwich, about to board
A schooner, for a place like this one,
I'd sooner stay at home, bored,
But comfortable, listening to Brian Eno.

I am damp to the innards of my watch.
Mosquitoes form a permanent halo,
Inches above the scalp. I should have got a Swatch,
Not a Seiko, and packed a shaving cream with aloe.

'You're gonna get your fucking head kicked in.'

After the match we walked home over cars
Most of us were yet to have our first shave
We could tell the time by deliveries of the Sun
Evening News *and* Standard *to the sweet shop*
News of the World *inked your hands the most*
On paper rounds we had the world at our fingertips

It was dirty and not all it was cracked up to be

We went into Georgetown on a mission.
Avoiding potholes in our drive from Timehri
Was an art.

We were at the head of a demonstration
That was illegal. For their temerity
They ate tar.

I broke my stave of greenheart;
My nunchakas too; ran out of missiles;
Was unhurt.

Unhurt by their prayers
Unhurt by their women screaming
Unhurt by their children crying
Unhurt by their elderly begging
Unhurt by them begging for mercy
Unhurt by the journalists
Unhurt by the cameras
Unfazed by this request from their government
For assistance to pacify these discontented
Ungrateful cruisin'-for-a-bruisin' souls

Rice flails and nunchakas know not
The difference between an East Indian
Or African head, between an afro –
That does not deflect a blow and possesses not

An iota of cushioning ability –
And a head of hair laid flat on the skull
By coconut oil: both heads crack
Or else are hard enough to crack back.

Do not wail
When you have brought my nunchakas
On your own head

Do not wail
For the teeth you have lost
To my rice flails

Do not wail
At all those days you will rot
In jail without bail

Banner, they say, Banner, give me a thing,
No? I have nothing to give but a thump
And a song – brand-new funky presidente
Yeah! We'll be forever loving Jah – or two.

Kaieteur, falling to powder puff;
Raggamuffin DJ days in Coldharbour Lane.
We sailed through the barrier at Woolwich
And pissed in the river as we passed Westminster.

Guyana
Not Ghana
Get it right
I am not a refugee
Who does not know his Africa
From his South America
His jungle from his desert
From his rainforest and savannah
Though all are dear to me

Stabroek market has a broken clock.
The time it tells is always right

Twice, then there is the time it doesn't tell.
Like how long this country can go without

Flour, rice, sugar, potato, corn,
Soap, oil, and anything else you care to list.

For as long as that clock can tell the time
And this whole market of shoppers not give a damn.

Back to back
In the face of adversity

Belly to belly
Rub your love all over me

We don't give a damn
This country dying slowly

I done dead already
Don't bother bury me

This is worse than the Front Line
In '75. Then, there was time for carnival.
Now is like a curse where there's no time
To measure cruelty and love is lavish

Or slavish, I mean, my watch is kaput,
Zippo, therefore I am mad, might is mad
Duties are madder, conscience is a cop-out
With my watch gone there's no dam.

No dam against the river
Swollen river muddy river

No dam against the burst dam
Otter dam mud dam

No dam against the likes of Father
Government dam police dam

No dam to get us out of this jam
Bible dam God dam

If a man acquired a cart, without a horse,
To sell mauby, shaved ice, coconut water,

By walking Georgetown, would it be a case
Of out the frying pan into the fire,

On account of Georgetown's choke and robbers
Lethal as coral snakes? A man could do worse

Than roam the capital blowing his own trumpet,
Like stay here and end up in a hearse.

But that would put Descartes before the Hobbes
We know and love; and that would put an end to verse.

Cart horse
Horse ice
Ice water
Water fire
Fire choke
Choke robber
Robber snake
Snake coral
Coral man
Man city
City love
Love verse
Verse hearse
Hearse trumpet
Trumpet love
Love cart
Cart love
Love fire
Fire love
Love water
Water love
Love love

Flood. Crops wasted away again.
Sun is a sign from far above.
We are ready to eat grubs
And the bark of trees,

When this army truck
Laden with tins and bread
Pulls into our compound –
A thank-you note from the President.

Make it funky – da dada dada da da
Make it funky
Provisions from the provider
President who has put the y
Back in our funk

Make it funky – da dada dada da da
Make it funky – domdom dom domdom
Funky President-e Yeah!

Thank my Uzi give me some ammo.
And some grease – Uzi food.
I have learned to tell the time by the sun

When I can see it in a clearing
Or free of cloud and by the way light
Lifts a long flowing skirt and crosses

The paddy field and the paddy bows
In suppliance. Light is greater than our Reverend.

Light hoods our eyes
Light creases our foreheads
Light makes our bones porous
Light darkens our skin
Light peels our heads
Light lifts us off the ground
Light puts us underground
Light forks our tongues
Light loosens teeth in our gums
Light tightens clitoris and scrotum

I tap the acacia tree for gum,
The coconut for milk,
The palm tree for wine.

I feel like that tapster Tutuola
Bumped off on page one, except
None have come or will ever tackle

This jungle to find me, so I tap, tap, tap,
Like Woody Woodpecker, minus the cackle,
While another drinks, drinks, drinks.

Woodpecker with one shoe
Tap tap tapping
On the windowless wood
A spider couldn't sound better
Morse none can decipher
Tell me the formula
For wine for milk for gum

If not a formula a recipe will do
If not a recipe
Say hello to my Uzi
In any language you please
I'll use your colourful quiff
As a puffed up cravat
And your beak for that unreachable itch

I eat from a leaf called the dasheen
My fingers are my knife and fork
I use grass to wipe my ass
Bathe beneath the clear cannon

Of a waterfall

Breeze towels my skin then a jolt
Wakes me from the one dream and I go
Work in the fields or tapping with a growl
In my belly and my belly on my mind.

My brains in my belly
My soul in my belly
My heart in my belly
My baby in my belly
My desire in my belly
My Muse in my belly
My God in my belly
My sins in my belly
My hopes in my belly
My dreams in my belly
My mother in my belly
My father in my belly
My wife in my belly
My children in my belly
My belly in my belly

The government truck that brings supplies
Is long overdue. Our leader got on the CB
And barked at some poor soul in Samson's
Office who wouldn't put Samson on the line.

Our leader threatened the wrath of God
Unless it rained bread, milk and wine
From the capital. Nunchakas, rice
Flails, greenheart clubs and my Uzi.

All the clouds are rice fields
Ready for harvest
All the clouds are coconut groves
Ripe for picking
All the clouds are sweet potatoes
Bubbling just below ground
All the clouds are a thousand plates
Brimming at an endless banquet
All the clouds are rolling by
Taking their promises elsewhere

Our leader likened our resolve to greenheart.
If this wood, he said, finger-wagging, wide-eyed,
Can find its way to London to buffer
Banks along the Thames, all the way – lover? –

From this interior we can surely establish
A toe-hold on the outskirts – under the skirts –
Or my name is not Jim Jones and we are not
The renowned People's Temple – we are not.

Blouse and skirts! Bumba cloth!
Rass cloth! Blood cloth!

Take the place of prayer
Our lexicon contracts to a hool

In a spool empty of cotton
A curse is as good as a song

Plate cloth! Kiss me rass!
Kiss me ass! Kiss me backside!

She is still with him or he with her.
She drinks directly from the fountain
Instead of from the trough. I miss her.

Her look says, you killed my husband
And brought me to this, therefore,
Sonny, you have zero hold over me.

She sits on her Mr Sheen hair beside him.
Love, there were others, will be others.

My love is true
Only as true
As I'm to you
As you're to me
As we're to us
And to ourselves
What is this love
What is this trust
What is this fuss
Without this love
Without this trust
Without this fuss
There is no me
There is no you
There is no us
Only a shell
An empty shell
An empty well
A silent drum
From here from now
From me to you
Till kingdom come
A measly crumb
Of what we are
Or could have been
No hosannas

Just bad manners
In bandannas
No myrrh
No manna
No frankincense
And all this life
A heavy load
A long sentence

There is a crop that can be grown in these hills
That won't wash away in the rain, that certain
Termites can't stomach, that fetches
A market price ten times that of rice.

Goodbye paddy field, good riddance sugar
Cane. Are we turning to good old bauxite?
No. Will it be prospecting for diamonds
Deeper in this quagmire like a pork-knocker?

When will we be delivered?
Answer
How long in this quagmire?
Answer
Why must the children suffer?
Answer
Where will we go from here?
Answer
What can you promise us now?
Answer
Will we still follow you?
Answer

No. This crop goes by several names:
Ganja, sinsimilla, marijuana, kaya,
Herb, ital, spliff, joint, fix, kale,
Spiritual food, the body of Christ,
The way to transubstantiation,
A means of escape from the shit-stem,
Food of the gods, opiate of the people;
Plant a seed, there is no sheriff to shoot.

You ask a man to watch the thing
He most craves
Watch but don't touch
Look but don't partake
Smell but don't taste
Imagine all he likes
But one false move . . .

What would Captain Steadman have done?
Not stick his finger up his bum and suck his thumb,

No, you get her to use her finger
And as for your thumb you tell her to suck
On the one between your legs –

He would have sung hymns of praises
For this heavenly crop. But if I catch
The first man partaking of that crop I'll shoot him.

This is not my body
Not mine to offer you
Nor my own property
Hotter than vindaloo
To get rid of easy
I sit in someone's pew
And pretend I am he
I walk in borrowed shoes
To get from A to B

Another's vindaloo
Another's wife warms me
Another's pew and shoe
Another's property
Another's me and you
No other life for me
No other wife or pew
No other me or you

Oh, dear leader, what is that laughter
Emanating from your Bedouin tent?
Is it, oh, is it the laugh of one I love?

O, dear leader, what are those fumes
Hanging like homemade weather above your quarters?

Could it be, oh, could it be the forbidden sinsimilla?

The blast of her laugh and that mushroom cloud
Devastates whole tracts of countryside in me.

Where there's smoke there's fire
Where there's jealousy there's fire
Where there's covetousness there's fire
Where there's excess there's fire
Where there's mockery there's fire
Where there's betrayal there's fire

There's no fire without smoke
There's no fire unless stoked
There's no fire without rope
Without hope without dope
Without fuel without Father

Take me to one of those English shires,
Douse me in petrol and set me ablaze.
I'd swap all this Mittelholzer
For just one Morning At The Office.

I had no mother to call a father,
No palace nor chalice, nor spliff,
No dreads to shake at despotic authority;
Just me, my unrequited love for her
With the hair and my trusted, rusty Uzi.

When poetry dies my love for you dies too
Or put another way my love for you
Can never die not as long as there's
Breath in me not as long as there's
Poetry for me to breathe my love

In order for my love for you to die
Not only must I be dead but so must you
And not only us two but verse too
And how can verse be dead when all
There is to say about our love has not been said

Has hardly begun to be said in fact
I take it back poetry is everlasting
Which is to say it exists outside of time
In turn our love as a poem outstrips time
And once time is given the slip there's no dying

There's only the life of the love to live
In this case us versus timelessness
Us two sharing this love that won't die
Even as we blink in our lives and expire
Our lives no longer than a blink in time

Our love no less than time no more
Than life itself us in that love
With nothing to lose if we lose our lives
Since that love has slipped from time
From death and lives as life itself

I try hard to think outside the scripture,
And to hear, when I think, a voice other than
Our illustrious leader's.

For a long time I walked around in a blank
And could do nothing else but stand quite still
When I tried to conjure

An image of a boa constrictor; a tiger
Tiger burning bright; a long-legged fly
But grossed *nada*.

Tiger come to warm up the party
Tiger here to jive in the dancehall
Tiger going to put the tickle back in you
Tiger bring the spice to put in your stew

Everybody want to be a tiger
Everybody afraid of the tiger
Everybody says he's friends with tiger
Everybody good to eat to the tiger

Don't cuddle a boa constrictor
Don't put your head in tiger's mouth
Don't wrestle with an alligator
Even if you have faith procure doubt

Many rivers to cross but I quibble
Over names: the Courentyne, Essequibo,
Potaro, Mazaruni, Demerara . . .

Dash me some o' that red rum, let's Banks
Up! Don't even bother with ice and water.
Ice! Buddy, I haven't seen ice in yonks.

The next man to turn up here will be boss,
Here, that is, with an ice-making machine,
Virginal to a mosquito's proboscis.

Mosquito one mosquito two
Mosquito jump in the old man's shoe

Mosquito three mosquito four
Mosquito knocking down our door

Mosquito five mosquito six
Mosquito eating its way through sticks

Mosquito seven mosquito eight
Mosquito pile us all on a plate

Mosquito nine mosquito ten
Mosquito nyam us all to death

If I had wings of a dove I would fly –
Where? Back to Brixton? Chattanooga?
Kalamazoo? I would settle for a nest
Comprised entirely of her Rapunzel plait.

But she lets it down for another,
And lies back on it like a mat,
And he wraps himself in what's
Left over and not a stitch between them;
And not a split end to spare me.

If love were a diet I'd be anorexic
for you
Thin as smoke on a blade of grass
for you
Light as a moonbeam on the iris
for you
Faint as a Dogstar at midday
for you
Dry-mouthed as a pothole in the Sahara
for you
Frond-lipped bruise-lipped puckered-lipped
for you
Static-skinned hangnail-ridden nose bleeding
for you
Wire my jaws warm water through straws
for you
Stone strapped to flatten my noisy belly
for you
Walkabout the four deserts of the Outback
for you
Nil by mouth nil by eyes nil by ears
for you
Rag and bone skin and bone bag of bones
for you
Less and less more or less less of me
for you

If L— were here what would he do?
Once in Edinburgh's Assembly Rooms
He got someone to look our way by merely
Willing it. Make Tikka look at me.

Her eyes never meet mine now.
Her stomach protrudes with twins
Who will appear with a full head of hair
And teeth that will have to be pulled.

I play a flute hollowed from bone
Bird beast or human I don't care
Old or young I'm indifferent
What eats me down to my skeleton
Is her with him night and day
Then I can't play can hardly think

L— would walk into our dear Father's shack,
His innermost, private and tastefully decorated
Sanctum

Whistling 'Dixie', and demand the immediate
Return of Tikka – were she yours to ask back
My chum –

Instead of dithering about infinite rows
Of marijuana with a huff and a puff and I swore
By gum

I won't inhale, meanwhile Father big-up my girl's
Belly, Banner, using her prodigious hair to towel
His cum.

When I don't smell marijuana
I smell semen
Neither issues from me

Instead I delight in a rainbow
That ended in a place
I could find

I stood in colours whose sweet taste
Silk touch rose smell arias
Made me the end of a rainbow

I drink from a jar steeped in tamarind.
The smooth head spends
Itself for a moustache and I ache for the Rhine
Or the hops of Kent.

Tikka's Paramaibo may be the rind
After-taste; a blend
I can no longer afford; that's the last time
My South gets burnt.

Thank that day in the vapour of the Mazaruni
When we played truant;
Thank the lasciviousness of Father for my ruin
That's permanent.

Imperceptibly ajar – that's me
My heart my tamarind heart
My love my tamarind love
My South my tamarind South
My Father my Father my Father

Let L— know there are men
Who walk these woods with their heads
Under their arms, diamonds grow
On vines, pork can be knocked
From the bloated ribs of a barrel;

Tell him the volcanic springs
Restore youth, and a man can lie
In a hammock, be inside a woman,
Not move a muscle and yet come
Over and over and over again.

Tell him what it takes to get him here.

I would rather be an alligator
In the Everglades
Or a fatty polar bear
Traipsing the North Pole
Or a photo-sensitive groundhog
In the Alleghenies
Or a racked-up moose on the loose
In the woods of Maine
Or a lone and wavy sandbar
In the Kalahari
Or the missing S
In Mississippi

Anything but this
Anywhere but here
Anyhow but now
Anyway but loose
Anyless but lost

If that doesn't stir his precious gonads

He's dead down there or else this

Hasn't got to him because the postage

Fell short or a kleptomaniac

For a postman has put my penned gem

In a pile in his spare room filed under

Fantasy or magical realism

Brewed from the heart of the hops of the South
Poured from a glass in a pub in the mouth

Rinsed from an ass in a room with a view
Gulped in the throat through a wall in a loo

Rolled off the wrist of a friend for a laugh
Stored in a tube just in case he got gassed

Stuck in the face of a nun on the run
Spread on the breast of a girl just for fun

Licked off the bum off the face off the chest
Left there to dry and to peel and to crust

Brewed in the balls of the crotch of a man
Poured from the cock in the cunt of woman

Poured in the ass in the mouth in the hand
Poured on the flesh on the hair on the land

I shared a girl with L—
Once and once only. We were out
Of our carnivorous brains on some Lebanese
Black in female company fit as a fox –
So-called on the performance poetry circuit –
Her friend was nowhere to be seen.

Before we knew it we were all clued
Into one another, minus our kits on the sofa bed,
No, futon, whatever, it started there and concluded . . .

M.Y.O.B. some things are best
Left to the imagination

For which there is as yet
No Inheritance Tax

'Yet' being the operative term

L— has rolled me one of his humongous
Spliffs. We take turns drawing until
The flame nibbles at our fingertips.
Then we get on my bike for the ride

From Peckham via the Elephant
To Coldharbour Lane, Brixton, for work.
A workshop of drums, poems, ackee and
Saltfish from the Front Line and brotherly love.

C-C rider
Master drummer
Rasta chanter
Word endorser
Brotherly love

Herbalist
Verbalist
Motorist
Masochist
Brotherly love

Salt and freshfish
Cat and dogfish
Flat and snakefish
Moon and sunfish
Brotherly love

L— asks me whether we will ever get there.
I ask him through my helmet and above the revs
To elucidate. He looks down at the front wheel

Warped by delta-9-tetrahydrocannabinol
And wonders if it should be up on the island
Dividing the road, like that, while the back

Wheel is on the road proper. I Vulcan-death-grip
The steering, though it points the wrong way.
When the island runs out, we are back on track.

My visor caught the sun
And bowled it back to the moon
In a flash a glint
A mere twinkle of an eye

My spokes churned the air
Into a twister
Wind was music to my ears
I twisted to its tune

Twisted and was lifted
Lifted and was transported
Transported and was altered
Altered and nearly died

Faith, boy, faith. I pointed that wheel
Like a plough whose coulter
Holds under pressure. That's what we felt –

Pressure; pushing up, L— said, when upset.
'This policeman, this policeman, this policeman
Keeps on beating me to death.' So I ups

And I leaves for the U.S. of A. The lady
With the ice cream cone, both green,
Or the Golden Gate? Neither, actually.

Ellis Island proved hellish
For C.L.R. proved particular-
ly brutish for all but a whale

A nation on the move rations
Love when it should shove
Hate overboard and let love stay

Hammer and sickle kept his mind in a cell
A cell for the sick without lock or key
Capitalism and the greenback keep me
Sick under lock and key keep me in hell

L—, why won't you write back!
Do you still reckon literacy
Is a Babylonian conspiracy!

Oh for just one line of your crab track.

One line is all I an' I brethren ask.
Then the mongoose will surely cuddle the asp,
Verily, my days will pass and I won't crack.

Like Tom who steps on a hoe
Jerry slips around
Like Coyote stuck with dynamite
Intended for Road Runner

Any Biff or Buff rough or scruff
Won't do 'Tie a yellow ribbon
Round the old oak tree . . .'
'Knock three times on the ceiling . . .'

Back to back, belly to belly,
Confusion of the deathbed transfer,
Fe fi fo fum, I smell the corpuscles

Of an American, Reverend, Seer, Daddy,
And Sir, if the States had the means to confer
Such an honour – they don't have the muscles.

There is cricket. Kanai or Kallicharran
Or Sobers at the crease and is pure runs.

I see stars you see wounds in that flag
I see red you see blood
I see sky you see blue
I see black you see white
I see stripes you see bars

You want your body draped in this flag
You wish to be anointed with its stars
You see its blue as an ocean of possible worlds
You swear the sun falls in that shade of red
Those stripes or bars are the straight necks of swans

L.B.W. is my greatest weakness.
L—'s was swinging, always swinging
For the boundary. Cricket baffles Reverend Jim,

Who has been known to kick a ball in his time.
Who can confirm or deny this?
No one in our midst,

Clobbered by ginseng
Root, brewed for a dry run, poured singing
Into a thousand enamel cups in this jungle clime.

Never trust a game where the players
Finish with clothes as fresh as when they began

Never trust a man who sells his books
To purchase flesh when he said he was vegan

Remember his name in your prayers
Whenever you say amen remember his looks

You see, Father had a vision, God help us.
He said what paradise
Was not; it was not this.

Temple members, he went on, would be first
To sample this
Actual paradise.

Then he got side-tracked onto some courageous
Act that was
Required of us.

But I switched off, remembering his last
Big promise
Resulted in this.

Keep him off those mushrooms
They're only giving him ideas

Most of them are deadly
For us if he has his way

Not that he needs any help
To dream up our nightmares

They just come to him natural
In the middle of the night and day

Daddy's particular brand
Of what I can only call his
Pseudopolyphilorosicrucianism
Is no more nor less than
Dalton's obfuscation
That goes something like this
Hurtyaburnyacutyamuch?

One addresses a grazed knee
One addresses the soul
One leaves you smiling
The other leaves you cold.

Come back Dalton
You left too soon
Bring more wisdom
Disguised as tomfoolery
All we have is a man
With a master plan
If you knew him like we do
You'd be biting your nails too
Down to the quick
Dalton come back

If I grow my hair into a modest,
Modish afro, I'd be six feet.
Out here I use a fork to comb
Out the knots.
        After a shower
At the white water falls I twirl
The ends so that they resemble
Tagliatelle.
        Father ordered me
To shave my head. As a punishment,
The razor was a broken bottle.

I didn't need those hairs
They were forked with neglect

I resembled Medusa
But lacked her appalling power

That bottle was no mirror
He looked me straight in the eye

I was the one who turned cold as stone
He slithered away in the razor grass

Jim Jones doesn't know his okra
From his bora;
His guava from his sapodilla;
His stinking-toe from his tamarind.

He will get us all into a jam,
A terrible pickle,
A big muckle,
An awful stew,

A humongous to-do,
A I am I and you are you
And all o' we is one,
And we all fall down.

Down to the bottom of the deep blue sea
Down to the centre of gravity
Down on our hands on our knees
Down on our luck unluckily

Girts – our word for an impromptu
Feast; hot cakes and cornsticks,
Washed down with mauby was utopia.

L— I wish you were here
To help me sing the way we sang
On the Front Line: I remember

When we used to sit and sing
Marley after Marley like anthems;
Us in our canvas yachting shoes.

We were undernourished
Those cornsticks were just flour and sugar

What filled us up was song
Three courses of song
Three square meals of songs
And a long line for leftover songs
In a three-legged vat on the floor
Ladled onto chipped enamel plates
Battered enamel cups with thanks

With praises hallelujahs amens
For this bounty from the great provider

Yachting shoes decorated with black biros
Lifted after we signed-on or signed our giros
At that cramped post office in Norwood.

And talk! As if talk were going for good,
About a Bill of Rights for these Isles of isthmus
As much as the Islets of Langerhans:

Would a Bill of Rights have saved those
Dozen young men killed in police custody?

Every red cent from that cashed cheque
Went from my hand to his then he
Would give me what he deemed
An appropriate sum for someone my age

Not enough to buy a round Daddy
But plenty for ice cream from the van
Crisps chocolate and orangeade
Me with hairs on my balls but what the heck

He was Father Daddy boss-man he-man
And I was scared of God

We had the notion that we'd walk
From Land's End to John o'Groats
Collecting signatures for a Bill
Of Rights, in our black and blue
Yachtings; collect enough names
To lay from one end of that land
To the other; then and only then
We'd hang up those shoes, what's
Left of them; that or never sing
Marley, Burning Spear, Tapazukie
As long as we drew English air . . .

Over a banana-skin climate
Over an orange-peel land
Over a blood-orange history
Over a star-apple kingdom
Over a pear-shaped people
Over a kiwi-fruit territory
Over a coconut-husk accent
Over a Granny-Smith culture
Over green-turnip weather
Over a courgette drama
Over an aubergine theatre
Over the potato moors
Over a split-pea valley
Over a channa wall
Over a grits seawall
Over a black-eyed pea sea
Over a sago moon
Over a penny-farthing lake
Over a runner-bean stream
Over banger-and-mash hills
Over a saveloy-and-chips Midlands
Over a vinegar rain
Over a blow-torch sun
Over a ketchup sun
Over a stethoscope wind

Over a sewer wind
Over a telescoped Island
Over a microscope Island
Over a shrink-wrapped Island
Over a gob-smacked Island
Over an I.O.U. nothing Island

Was it the stuff of liming on street corners?
Idle gaff? Light labrish?

A Bill of Rights for the Front Line
As much as for the boys from the Blackstuff,
For Glasgow's tenement
Blocks and the Shankhill Road,
For Tiger Bay and Millwall's Den?

A Bill of Rights, we vowed, before the outing
Of our lights.

Turn those lights down low
Fox clad in sheep's wool
Eyes wide as those of an owl
My head spins on a spool
A thought begins then loops
Back on itself in slow
Motion and seems to glow
In darknesses that loom
Wheel and turn down low

To conjure something
From Cordelia's nothing;
To move the weightless
And therefore weighted
Mind on silence; to keep
That sleeping head,
In Auden, human.

L— our foreheads
Shone when we ducked
From the shop front
Into the dawn light,
Light beginning, yes,
In the eaves of all places,
With a gloss finish
Stretched out from A
To Z.

Tarmac after a pinging shower
Ponged of the past
Heat from the village bakery
Waters the mouth of every child
In sight in earshot in touch
In taste of its Pied Piper pull

And once the baker came to the gate
Laden with a tray of hot cakes
After his wife gave birth to twins

Cast your eye down that street
Steam in an alphabet of S's rises
Off a loaf London long London wide

Tikka becomes a mother, at 2.45 a.m.
I hear her curse the Reverend
As the midwife urges her to push.

Silence builds this edifice, crammed
Into the longest while, that a cry demolishes;
Then laughter through tears; then the Reverend

Curses my name, storms out and finds me,
Wrestles my Uzi from me, aims,
Fires once, twice, but it's jammed.

Clickety clack
Clippety clop
Hoppety hop
Stoppety stop
Droppety drop
Smackety smack
Slappety slap
Kickety kick
Stoppety stop
Droppety drop
Flippety flop
Fuckety fuck
Moppety mop
Punchety punch
Spittety spit
Grabbety grab
Stoppety stop
Droppety drop
Bloodety blood
Bleedety bleed
Droppety drop
Stoppety stop

'Get out and take her with you
And the damned baby.
If I lay eyes on you again boy
These hands will kill you.'

'Father, the child may be her husband's.
I lay with her one time on the banks
Of the Mazaruni, just the once.
Her husband must look a lot like me.'

Don't argue with Father
Argue with the weather
Don't argue with Father
Argue with the savannah
Don't argue with Father
Argue with the forest
Don't argue with Father
Argue with the river
Don't argue with Father
Argue with alligators
Don't argue with Father
Argue with yellow fever
Don't argue with Father
Argue with coral snakes
Choke and robbers piranahs
Poisoned arrows scorpions
But don't argue with Father

I addressed his receding backside
Shielding my face from blows
His bodyguards measured out.

One of them filched my watch.
Another my newly discarded Uzi.
I pleaded to their receding backs

That my timepiece and gun had ceased
Functioning since we got here, seized
Up by moisture, useless to all humanity

But me and my materialist sentimentality.
How long did I watch and wait for
The moment when they'd concur?

Disable the alarm of me
Strip the trimmings of me
Rip the radio of my head
Black out my headlights
Smash my tail lights
Puncture my tyres
Flog my wheels
Cut up my leather interior
Graffiti paint my exterior
Leave the gutted shell of me for dead
Walk away all smiles and high fives
Leave the fractured skull of me for dead

The one with my watch pressed
It to his left ear, paused to listen,
Then to his right, and again, paused,

Before he pitched it with disdain.

The one with my Uzi was more –
Shall I say – scientific? He didn't pore
Over it. He pointed it at me, fired, saw
That it really and truly was

Jammed, then threw it in my rough direction.

I scrambled on all fours,
Recovered both from the tall razor
Grass, hugged them in the crook of my neck,
Like they'd been born to me this second.

My children lost abracadabra

Then restored in a flash 'Just like that'
As Tommy Cooper said to camera

Cuddle them cradle them squeeze them tight
Let them know might is not always right

Love conquers flesh and bone and spirit
My Uzi and my watch have proved it

When I looked up
She was standing there,
He arms full of the cowled child.

'Shouldn't you be lying down?'
She smiled and walked off towards
What I knew to be the Mazaruni.

I followed. She stopped and said,
Without turning to face me or even
Swivelling her head to look round,

That I could not come, not where
She was going, in a tone that turned
My legs to stone and left my head in a stew.

Savannah encircles this forest
River and a high tide loop-the-loop
I seem to be standing on my head
Ambulant on cushions of banked cloud
With the moss on the stones shaving me
Now the whole scrambled scene giddies up
As if that stewing pot has been gripped
By two hard working hands and shaken
Not just stirred lifted and roughly tossed
Up and down left and right all around

When I came to, I was in the throes
Of yellow fever and still in Jonestown.

So much for my part as a Black Jacobin.
Tikka was gone with our daughter or son,

While I burned up in a hide-out
From Father, who would kill

Me on sight. From where I holed-up
I could hear his sermons well

Into the night, over the p.a.
And the swift Trades, about that para-

dise reserved for Temple people
Who kept faith in him and hope.

And suppose I happen to go mad
Testosterone driven gonad
That I am would she be glad or sad

Our eponymous protagonist
Figures prominently in this
He tells us we are his business

I was able to keep down
A bowl of cornmeal porridge
Laced with hot goat's milk.

This was taken as a sign
That the fever had subsided
And was now on the out and out.

Feed me more of that corn,
But don't warm the goat –
Or should it be harm? – milk.

Milk cold or hot
  Milk from Father
Milk cow and goat
  Milk from Father
Milk at morning
  Milk from Father
Milk at evening
  Milk from Father
Milk sweet or sour
  Milk from Father
Milk gall bitter
  Milk from Father

The yellow fever in my veins
Goes tick-tock, tick-tock.

I mistake it for my wrecked watch.

The yellow fever in my veins
Is loaded like my Uzi,

But isn't choosy unlike my Uzi,

And might, one of these days, flare
Up and obliterate yours truly.

I watch the fever
The fever watches me
I'm a tree on fire
A burning baccilli tree

Either I will be ashes
Or I'll become a bird
Scattered in these marshes
Spread all over the world

Once, as I waited for my luggage,
At Piarco,

These two strapping young things
Wrapped in Kente

Bounced over to me and asked
If I was Salif Keita

Or his twin
And would I sing –

cock-a-doodle-do,
cock-a-doodle-do.

At least at Timehri
I had anonymity
On my side and beside me
If you count my stout Uzi

Ah but to carry a tune
As though it were weightless
Melanin in skin cells
Or red eyes in a night picture

I am neither and on the rare
Occasions when I sing
I like to think I sound
Like, wait for it, Nina Simone.

For instance, when I take a shower
Down at the Falls . . .
Nina Simone doing that number
By Cohen, better than Cohen,

Called 'Suzanne',
At the Holiday Inn,
Of all places, Islamabad,
In Bhutto's Pakistan.

In Muzaffarabad
We drove above cloud
On a steep windy road that had
No lane dividers no hard
Shoulder nor barrier

Birds hung in the valley below
Our chests heaved
Our nostrils flared
The driver sang with one hand
On the steering wheel

And the other over his heart
Some Mohammed Rafi
Famous in these parts
For how and what he
Made love and time into art

We wound our way up,
Through cloud,
To surface at the top
Of one of the Roraimas,

Ate a lunch of cold meats,
Toileted with our backs
To the four winds,
Took snapshots,

Of each other,
Of the panorama,
Piled stones one on another,
Then wound our way down again.

Look as I did
There was no sign of the border
Bush was unbroken
Rivers twisted to the four winds
A sudden shower
Crossed the entire vista
In one sweep of shadow and light
Covering all things equally
With its mineral bath

My fever is like a watch
Or that climb up a Roraima

It winds itself up to a pitch
Then winds itself down,

Down to a simmer or simper.

As it winds up I go down
On my blue-black, sore back

With my mind on my Uzi
And my Uzi on my mind.

As it winds down I get up,

Up on top of the world.
And I'm giddy, black and blue

And sore from that beating
The Reverend's guards gave me.

I could play the maracas
In a club in Caracas

Or become a surveyor
In this forest interior

I'm close to Venezuela
Closer to vain Mahalia

Jackson's bluesy soul gospels
Closer still to H's Palace

Today was a good day.
I kept down all my sago
But the blasted porridge
Seemed full of beady eyes,
Like tadpoles, like peacock
Feathers, like life.

And that bowl rimmed in red,
As that marker the fever
Pencilled round my lids.
Everything my eyes touched
Seemed about to burst into flames.

The feeling is with him
When you leave the room
You no longer exist

So you spend all your time
Trying to get
An audience with him

You're like one of Mahon's
Withering mushrooms
In a Disused Shed . . .

With no chance of catching
A chink of light
Leaning towards what you

Believe to be
A light source
Some imminent presence

You would change but
Everyone around you
Does the same

Carrion crows circled and circled
Reluctant, on account of me, to land.

Carrion ... so pungent, there was a taste
I spat and spat to expel,

But it stayed and moistened
My nose as much as my eyes.

The red stencilled round my lids
Ran but instead of tasting salt,

I tasted bitter: I had no control
Over the contortions of my face,

The gyrations of my body,
The stamping like bare feet on hot coals.

You are face to face
But he is elsewhere
You tell him you can't
Live in this place
And what does he say?
His hands appear
To sweep flies
That are not there
From his face
His eyes look past
You as though
You were a screen
Sheltering something
Of interest beyond
His wrinkled face
Wants this noise
Before him
To stop soon
You leave his company

Saying your name
Aloud along with
Descartes' dictum
Worked out by him
In an oven

I was bleeding from my eyes
Some thing supplied to my tearducts
By my ineluctable gall bladder.

Hadn't it been removed at King's
Or Guy's? The stones put in a jar
So that when I opened my eyes in recovery

The first thing I clapped eyes on
Wasn't my sweetheart or even L—,
But them, staring back, admonishingly.

Rain through sun and I hear Father
Cut grass smell and I hear Father
Axe splitting wood and I hear Father
Sugar cane in my mouth and I hear Father
Ripe guava smell and I hear Father
Dry husk torn from coconut shell – Father

Donkey bray at midday and I hear Father
Dissipating jet trail and I hear Father
Ankle clutch of a vine and I hear Father
Dry eye baby cry and I hear Father
Mist in the trees and I hear Father
High tide grinding down stones – Father

Tamarind on my tongue and I hear Father
Gall in my mouth and I hear Father
Chest burn heart burn and I hear Father
Air too thick for lungs and I hear Father
Bone brittle bone sore and I hear Father
Big man bawl big woman pull hair – Father

Could I have two gall bladders?
There's one for the books.

Shadows cast from those crows strengthen.
Does that mean they're lower?

Or has the sun intensified?
Nothing's between sun and me but crows.

If they would be still for a moment,
I could pretend they were clouds.

Shame is the sweat on the back of the neck
Shame is the hair stood on end on a neck
Shame is the key on a string round the neck
Shame is the knot of a noose round the neck
Shame is the wrung and then strung up high neck
Shame is a pulse under skin round the neck
Shame is the cut artery in the neck
Shame is a bruise or a bite on the neck
Shame is a hole for a tube down the neck
Shame is a head that's too big for a neck
Shame is a head that's too small for a neck
Shame is the skin that's too loose on the neck
Shame is the strain looks like strings on the neck
Shame is a lump in the throat and the neck
Shame is the ring piled on ring round a neck
Shame is the shame of the shame of the neck

The lump under my pillow
Is my Uzi.

The lump in my breast pocket
Over my heart
Is my comatose watch.

The lump in my throat
That I can't swallow
Away, no matter how hard
I try, is what?

Strain into string
Ring piled on ring
Knot of a noose
Skin that's too loose
Lump in the throat
Neck of a stoat

Tikka watches over me.
I share a crib with our baby.

Tikka's foot rocks the cradle.
Tikka sings and weaves a hammock,

The hammock we will lie in, stuck
Together, that the Trades will handle,

Ever so gently, so that as we break
At the same time, our baby won't wake.

But I do wake, on every occasion,
With my fever as my only companion.

And now this carrion and these crows.
And now their strengthening shadows.

Not sure which of the two suns
I feel warming my brittle bones

Is which. The fever low in the sky,
Or the fever inside my marrow.

Damn sure I don't care for either.

I am the black general, Toussaint
L— is my most trusted Lieutenant.

We are standing on the promontory
In Greenwich Park, facing an easterly

Direction, one foot either side the meridian,
A foot in each camp, as it seemed then:

Black and white, urban and rural, Salman's
East, West, romantic and cynic rolled into one.

I left my village
And my village girl
For a town my age
Which is no age at all

I am stirring pepper
In a pepper pot
Memories for casrep
Memories for stock

'Something is happening
And you don't know what it is.'

You're curious but you feign
A studied nonchalance.

'Señor, señor, can you tell me
Where we're heading . . .' The pots

Of broth are brought to the boil
Then left to simmer and stirred

And watched over, as they bubble,
Bubble, toil and trouble.

Bubble, bubble, toil and trouble
Father, never any good at Scrabble,
Turned to the Bible
Then away from the Bible
Into Scriptures scripted by himself.

Scriptures scripted by the gifted
Is one thing, in the hands of the mediocre
And the wicked, it's slimy as okra,
a.k.a. Lady's Fingers (confused with bora).

'Make my funk the P-funk.'
He hummed as he stirred the vat
Full of uncarbonated, reconstituted
Kool-Aid, laced with cyanide.

It was the ganja singing, not him.
He'd earlier rolled something more akin
To a spring roll, it was so neat and fat,
Than a joint, and kept it all to himself.

Who dubbed the deadly concoction
Corentyne Thunder cocktail?
A liquid bullet? But told
The unsuspecting children
Daddy-Kool, and the old, elixir
To the gateway of heaven?

Who would have the honour
To blow out Father's ingenious
Brains first, then his paltry
Own almost immediately afterwards?

We tossed for it. I called. I lost.
That coin had heads on both sides.
Just as the flat sides of a cutlass
Stung all the same whichever side
Father used to slap our behinds.

We had to say thank you every time,
And smile, as for a camera
About to take the best aspect
Of ourselves, about to save our souls
For posterity, say cheese.

For a group about to embark
On an excursion to God's theme park

Everyone sure sounds miserable:
Groans, moans, wails, irascible

Gunfire, prayer, voices in a mess
As they beg for mercy or forgiveness

Or both. Mercy from what thing?
Forgiveness for what wrongdoing?

I am on my back.
I keep nothing down.
Something vile is ladled
Into my craw. I swallow,
Lie back and have hardly
Settled when I retch
Bringing up all, I mean
All, every last scrap
Of that magic potion
From that cauldron
Of our Reverend's
Means to paradise.

Jim Jones in his heaven.
A gross of virgins
Impregnated by him,
Lie dead and swollen
With child.
                    Dead
And swollen people
Scattered everywhere.
Jim Jones in his heaven.
Him Temple haunted
By a thousand ghosts.

'Is it sent out naked on the road',
The soul, that is, wilfully sent abroad,

Snuffed, dishonourably discharged from you,
From life; or must it wait in a queue,

Suspended in a web, until the dear,
Forgiving, all-devouring spider

Returns; felt on that tremulous porch,
Like a faint echo, a long approach,

Long before it's properly heard or seen,
Like that long desert take, shot by Lean.

What would the Captain have done in my shoes?
Pooped his pants, just like me. I don't care
Who you are, when cyanide starts to work

On the diminutive frame of a child,
That child doesn't simply cry, it screams,
A high-pitched rend of a scream and is cut

Dead as quick as it began, leaving what
Dear Tom Paulin would call (wouldn't he?)
A rain (is it r-a-i-n-e or r-e-i-g-n?) of turds.

These are bodies lying on mud floors
In huts; on the grass; around dead fires;
In final embraces throughout
The neat wooden walkways;
On every clearing; and from now on
By the banks of the Potaro, the Mazaruni,
Essequibo, Corentyne, Demerara.
At Timehri. Quetzalcoatl,
Tell me this is not so.

I feel so far from Chattanooga.
Kalamazoo may as well be on the moon.
Brixton is less real than a fiction.

L—, I can trust, but where is he?
Not among these bloated bodies.
Not among these swollen banks.

And today a little less in my head.
Though no less in my ticker.
Or should that be Tikka?

Georgia on my mind. Carter on bass.
No drums, no cymbals, not even a piano.
Just Carter on bass and Georgia on my mind.

The snake that consumed the bird's egg
In one gulp, ate its better half:
Quetzalcoatl on the ground on his belly,

Now a mere shadow on the ground
As he circles on less than a wingbeat
High over these monocot trees.

Come back past philology
And all that. Come back, too,
Enid Blyton, all is forgiven,
Well, almost all. Baby
Come back!

You said you had to go.
You did not have to go.
Come back! Dom, dom, dom,
Dom, dom, dom; baby come back!

Tikka sits on her hair
Somewhere not here

L— sips on a brew
Somewhere not here

I wish I had my fever
Somewhere not here

I wish those crows circled
Somewhere not here

A brew is it sonny? And would that be
A Whitbread by any chance?

Not by the hairs on my chinny chin chin.

Oh what is that sound?

Tick-tock, tick-tock. Smeee!
Get that thing away from me!

My heart as regular as clockwork?
No? Not my Seiko?! Good be Jesus!
It can't be! No! It can't be!

A fucking miracle, that's what.
I'm going to get up and walk
Right outta this place,
Inna dis ya time, as LKJ would say.

Now for my trusted Uzi.
Those crows, for instance.
Rat-a-tat-tat! Rat-a-tat-tat!
Two fucking miracles, no less.

Mudhead. That's me. The midday sun
Shucked me once too often. Skites!
Banner! Give me a chance, no?

I drank from the cauldron
But I am not back to back,
Belly to belly. I was fed

Tupelo honey. Death in the form
Of a fever already had a hold
On me, on my mind and my mudhead.

I am in a painting by Bosch.
If I sneeze or cough
The whole scene will dissolve
And the insubstantial pageant . . .

But no. That carrion crow
Sprouted wings that swivel,
And instead of a caw, caw,
The rotaries of a helicopter.

The first thing I do
In my first hotel since Jonestown
Is throw out the Gideon.
I'd rather read the telephone
Directory, and do, scanning it,
For a name I know, or think I know.

God is in His heaven
While the Devil has his way
With us, with or without butter;
It was a case of rock me again
And again, and again, and again,
And again, and again.

I write by a bare 100 watt
Bulb. No shade. None
I could find pleased.
Not one out of thousands.

Shelves of lamp shades
In every conceivable shade
Of colour, but not one
Made for me. Not one.

Not one survives to tell the tale.

Is nothing sacred?
The question is, can anything
Purport to be sacred?

The People's Temple was sacred.
Oh, pl-ease! Bear with me.
This jungle is sacred.

Yet it, too, has its price.
L— is cut down by the big C;
My letters to him, all wait for me.

I go to Forest Hill, near the Horniman
Museum, to find L—'s grave.

Until the philosophy that treats one race
Inferior to another is finally,
And permanently, discredited . . .

I hear Marley and see him,
Not far from here, at the Crystal
Palace bowl, when I should hear,
Or at least see, Haile Selassie.

Quetzalcoatl, bled of all meaning.
Was it something I did or said?

Pawpaw fed to me, slice by slice in
A garden of bonsai trees ranged on a dais,

In the southernmost point of a contintent.

Without L—, the baba and my lady,
I feed on bile that is bitter to the gall.

Snake or bird, snake and bird, I crawl,
And when it pleases me, I fly.

I picked up the rockers
Tapazukie
Implored me not to throw
Away;
I love to rockers
Strictly rockers
Today,
Kris-kris,
Kris rockers, yeah,
Kris-kris, kris rockers.

The vitamin he made us take –
N-di-isopropyl-glucuronate
In a rehearsal of white night
Equalled a placebo
Or writing read in a mirror –
'Draw o coward' and 'madam'.

L— is dead. Tikka's as good as.
Our child remains faceless to me.

When I walk, it's over a thousand
Dead; so I stand on the spot
Staring at one place
Whose pattern, I pray, will not
Scramble into a town full of dead.

Nothing passes my lips that is not ital
By which I mean salt-free

Not a scavenger of the earth –
Earth hath nothing more fair –

Free of additives and preservatives.

They send their biggest and baddest
To inject me. I stand and face them

But they Sumo-throw me on my back,
Plunge the needle through my jeans

Back out, wide-eyed and breathy.

You guessed right. My new address –
Denmark Hill. From my room
On the locked ward, I hear trains
Clackety-clack to somewhere
I can't go: Chattanooga, Kalamazoo
Or even Timbuctoo. Not Karaudanawa.

I am not a pork-knocker.
Nor have I hollowed an enemy's bone
Into a flute. I am made dizzy
By the very thought of a Gideon,
Never mind the unexpurgated version.

'I don't know, I don't know
Why they got people bad-minded so.'

'Oh lawd mih bucket gat a ole
In dih centa
And if yuh tink ah tellin lie
Jook yuh finga

Brown skin gal stay home an mine baby
Brown skin gal stay home an mine baby

I am going away to the U.S.A.
And if I doan cum back
Throw way dih damn baby'

Click my heels three times
And abracadabra, Bob's your uncle,
Home sweet home.

I cross the threshold alone,
Not Chattanooga, nor Kalamazoo,
Nor all the good vibes of the Front Line

Can drag me back. Augusta
Is nearer to Canada
Than America, and it is home to me.

I post No Soliciting on my door,
Request that no advertising letters
Come through my letter box and ride
My mower round my one and a half acres.

My friend visits when I can afford her.
She calls me one of her regulars.
I get a discount for her love.
She says I am a very good lover.

I keep a stave of greenheart wood
Against intruders – no rice flails,
Nunchakas, knuckle-busters allowed.
My Uzi is classified as an 'implement

For hunting'; my greenheart stave doubles
As a walking stick. I have arthritis
In my left ankle, left knee and wrist.
The authorities are none the wiser.